I Cannot Keep My Hands Off You

Exploring Anxious-Preoccupied Attachment Style

Have you ever wondered why you feel and behave the way you do in your romantic relationship? Maybe your partner has said something like, **'I'm exhausted from constantly reassuring you!'** If that sounds familiar, pick up this book and read a few pages. It's all about *you*—specifically, the part of you that operates automatically. Think of it as **Your Owner's Manual for Your Relationship Brain.**

What is your attachment style? Before purchasing this book, please check your attachment style with the quiz on page 4.

You can also take the online attachment style quiz here (5min): <u>www.emikochibana.com</u>"

Disclaimer

The characters in the stories presented here are entirely fictional, and any resemblance to real persons, living or deceased, is purely coincidental. If you have any questions or concerns, please feel free to contact me directly.

This book does not substitute for professional opinion, diagnosis, therapy interventions or medical advice. If necessary, please seek the support of a qualified professional.

Emiko Chibana (www.emikochibana.com)

Table of Contents

Attachment Style
Self-Assessment Questionnaire

1. Strongly Disagree,
2. Disagree
3. Somewhat Disagree
4. Neutral
5. Somewhat Agree
6. Agree
7. Strongly Agree

Section A

I find it easy to get close to others.

1	2	3	4	5	6	7

StronglyDisagr   Strongly Agree

I feel comfortable depending on others and having others depend on me.

1	2	3	4	5	6	7

StronglyDisagr   Strongly Agree

I don't worry about being abandoned or about someone getting too close to me.

1	2	3	4	5	6	7

StronglyDisagr   Strongly Agree

I feel confident that my partner will be there for me when I need them.

1	2	3	4	5	6	7

StronglyDisagr   Strongly Agree

I enjoy a balance of intimacy and independence in relationships.

1	2	3	4	5	6	7

StronglyDisagr   Strongly Agree

Section B

I often worry that my partner doesn't really love me or won't want to stay with me.

1	2	3	4	5	6	7

StronglyDisagr   Strongly Agree

I tend to be very sensitive to my partner's moods and actions.

1	2	3	4	5	6	7

StronglyDisagr   Strongly Agree

I often need reassurance from my partner about their feelings for me.

1	2	3	4	5	6	7

StronglyDisagr   Strongly Agree

I sometimes feel that I put more into the relationship than my partner does.

1	2	3	4	5	6	7

StronglyDisagr   Strongly Agree

I am uncomfortable being without close relationships.

1	2	3	4	5	6	7

StronglyDisagr · Strongly Agree

Section C

I want to be close to others, but I find it difficult to trust them completely.

1	2	3	4	5	6	7

StronglyDisagr · Strongly Agree

I am afraid that I will be hurt if I allow myself to get too close to others.

1	2	3	4	5	6	7

StronglyDisagr · Strongly Agree

often feel that I don't deserve the love and support of others.

1	2	3	4	5	6	7

StronglyDisagr · Strongly Agree

I struggle with wanting intimacy but being afraid of it at the same time.

1	2	3	4	5	6	7

StronglyDisagr · Strongly Agree

I find myself withdrawing when relationships become too intense.

1	2	3	4	5	6	7

StronglyDisagr   Strongly Agree

Section D

I prefer not to depend too much on others or have others depend too much on me.

1	2	3	4	5	6	7

StronglyDisagr   Strongly Agree

I am comfortable without close emotional relationships.

1	2	3	4	5	6	7

StronglyDisagr   Strongly Agree

I feel that I am a strong, independent person.

1	2	3	4	5	6	7

StronglyDisagr   Strongly Agree

I sometimes feel that relationships are more trouble than they are worth.

1	2	3	4	5	6	7

StronglyDisagr   Strongly Agree

I prefer to keep my feelings and problems to myself.

1	2	3	4	5	6	7

StronglyDisagr   Strongly Agree

Your Attachment Style: Result & Interpretation

Section Totals: After completing the questionnaire, calculate the total score for each section.

Section A	Section B	Section C	Section D

High Score in Section A: *Secure Attachment Style*

A high score in Section A suggests that you have a secure attachment style. This style is often considered the foundation for healthy relationships, providing emotional stability and resilience. Individuals with secure attachment can maintain balanced, fulfilling connections with others through empathy, patience, and understanding. While this series does not offer a book specifically dedicated to securing attachment, we discuss it as the ideal model throughout all our publications. We encourage you to explore these sections for further insights into cultivating and maintaining this healthy attachment style.

High Score in Section B: *Anxious-Preoccupied Attachment Style*

A high score in Section B indicates a strong tendency towards an anxious-preoccupied attachment style. If you find yourself frequently seeking reassurance in relationships and feeling insecure, this orange book was created with your needs in mind. We hope it serves as a resource for healing and helps guide you towards building stronger, more secure relationships.

High Score in Section C: *Dismissive-Avoidant Attachment Style*

A high score in Section C reflects a tendency towards an avoidant attachment style. Individuals with this style may find it challenging to depend on others or open emotionally. To support your journey, we recommend the book titled *"If You Love Me, Set Me Free: Exploring Dismissive-Avoidant Attachment Style."* This book, with its purple cover, is designed to help you understand your attachment style and provide strategies to foster deeper, more meaningful connections.

High Score in Section D: *Fearful-Avoidant Attachment Style*

A high score in Section D indicates a strong inclination towards a fearful-avoidant attachment style. This style can lead to a complex push-pull dynamic in relationships, often driven by both a desire for connection and a fear of closeness. For further guidance, we suggest reading *"Push Me Away & Pull Me Close: Exploring Fearful-Avoidant Attachment Style"* This book, with its green cover, aims to help you navigate these conflicting emotions and work towards healthier, more secure relationships.

Introduction: What Is Attachment Injury?

Attachment injury refers to a type of psychological pain that arises when core attachment needs in childhood are not fully met, particularly in relationships with primary caregivers. The depth and impact of these injuries can be profound, often difficult to capture fully in words. In the sections that follow, we explore various factors and situations through case studies presented in story form. These examples are designed to help clarify the concept of attachment injury, and we hope they offer you valuable insights along your journey.

As you read these stories, if something resonates deeply with you, it may be an indication of unhealed attachment injuries within yourself. You may have tried to cover up the pain or convinced yourself that "everything is fine," yet these unresolved injuries can continue to influence your unconscious thoughts, emotions, and behaviors in daily life. Confronting these injuries can feel overwhelming and isolating at times. However, simply acknowledging the pain may provide a sense of relief and the first step toward healing. Remember, you do not have to navigate this path alone. Therapy can be a powerful way to begin the healing process.

If your therapist has recommended this book, it signifies that they are ready to guide you on this healing journey. Our hope is that the insights here will help you understand why certain thoughts or behaviors emerge in your relationships and offer you a way to break free from these patterns. Building healthier, more secure connections is entirely possible. By learning and practicing these approaches, healing will gradually take place. We sincerely hope this book becomes a helpful companion on your path toward emotional well-being.

Factors Contribute to Anxious-Preoccupied Attachment

The anxious-preoccupied attachment style, sometimes called ambivalent attachment, is often shaped by unstable caregiving relationships or inconsistent emotional responses during childhood. Several key factors that contribute to this attachment style include, but are not limited to:

Inconsistent Caregiver Responses:

When caregivers oscillate between warmth and indifference or become overly involved at times and distant at others, it creates confusion for the child. The unpredictability of receiving love and care leads to heightened anxiety, causing the child to feel they must constantly seek reassurance and approval from their caregiver.

Overprotection or Over-involvement:

If caregivers are overly protective, limiting a child's autonomy, the child may struggle to build self-confidence or a sense of security. This can result in a heightened dependency on the caregiver, with the child becoming excessively preoccupied with gaining their love and approval.

Unstable Home Environment:

In homes marked by frequent conflict, divorce, or instability, children are more likely to feel insecure in their relationships with caregivers. When a parent's emotional state is unpredictable or unstable, it can lead the child to perceive love as fleeting, contributing to the development of an anxious attachment style.

Emotional Manipulation or Control by Caregivers

If caregivers rely on their children to fulfill their emotional needs or expect the child to provide emotional support, the child may suppress their own feelings to maintain the relationship. These dynamic fosters dependency, as the child becomes focused on seeking approval and reassurance from the caregiver, making anxious attachment more likely.

Caregiver's Unstable Mental State

Caregivers who struggle with their own mental health challenges, such as anxiety, depression, or high levels of stress, may provide inconsistent emotional responses. This unpredictability can cause the child to feel unsafe or unsure, leading to attachment behaviors that are overly focused on seeking comfort and reassurance.

When these patterns persist, children may grow into adults who display heightened dependency in their relationships, often fearing abandonment and experiencing insecurity. The anxious-preoccupied attachment style, characterized by these emotional challenges, can continue to shape interactions and relationships well into adulthood.

In the next section, we present short stories that reflect the experiences of children and how attachment injuries manifest. These fictional stories aim to provide a deeper understanding of the psychological effects of different attachment dynamics.

Please note that the characters and episodes in these stories are entirely fictional and not based on real individuals or experiences.

Story 1: Alcohol Dependency and Unstable Parenting

Sara grew up with a mother who struggled with alcohol dependency. At times, her mother was loving and caring, but at other times, she was completely absent both physically and emotionally. Sara developed the habit of trying to predict her mother's state each day when she came home from school. On good days, her mother would help with homework and prepare dinner, but on bad days, Sara had to manage on her own, sometimes going to bed hungry. This instability planted a belief in Sara that relying on others was pointless, and that life inherently meant difficulty. As an adult, Sara avoids trusting and relying on others, and in romantic relationships, she constantly feels doubt and jealousy, experiencing intense emotional ups and downs. Her childhood experiences with her mother caused deep attachment injuries, making it difficult for her to form stable relationships.

Story 2: Emotional Neglect and Decreased Empathy

John was raised by parents who were constantly busy with work and didn't express emotions. They saw emotional expression as a weakness and often ignored or dismissed John's feelings, telling him things like, "Be stronger" or "You're too sensitive," without truly acknowledging how he felt. John learned to hide his emotions and, without receiving comfort or validation, internalized the belief that his feelings were unimportant and had no value. As an adult, John became emotionally numb, sometimes confused about what he was feeling, and his ability to empathize with others remained underdeveloped. As a result, he struggles to deepen relationships and often feels isolated. The very concept of caring about others' emotions seems absent in his interactions. John's childhood emotional neglect caused significant attachment injuries, preventing him from developing empathy.

Story 3: Emotional Absence Due to Parental Illness

Anna grew up with a mother who suffered from severe depression. Her mother often couldn't get out of bed, and there were many times when they couldn't have normal conversations or interactions as mother and daughter. Even when Anna achieved good grades or had fights with friends, she had no one to share these experiences with. Her father, frustrated by coming home to a house with no cleaning, no laundry done, and no meals prepared, began having an affair with another woman. At home, he withdrew into his own world, avoiding emotional connection with Anna, and minimized conversations with her. As an adult, Anna believes that being in a loving, intimate relationship defines her self-worth, and unconsciously associates not having a partner with being unlovable. Her relationships are often dependent, and she constantly seeks reassurance from her partner. She suffers from low self-esteem and frequently feels she is undeserving of love. For Anna, the presence of a romantic partner equates to her value as a person, making it unbearable for her to be single. Her mother's depression and father's emotional absence caused deep attachment injuries, making it difficult for Anna to feel emotionally secure as an adult.

Story 4: Losing a Parent Due to an Accident or Illness

When Michael was seven years old, his mother left for work and never returned. She had been involved in a tragic car accident. Initially, Michael couldn't comprehend the concept of his mother's death, leading to confusion and emotional turmoil. His father tried to support him emotionally, but having never been comfortable with emotional engagement himself, combined with the need to continue working, Michael was left feeling abandoned and alone. This isolation was deeply painful for him. As an adult, Michael fears losing loved ones and constantly worries about when he might feel that overwhelming sense of loneliness again. His childhood loss caused severe attachment injuries, leading to heightened anxiety and fear in his romantic relationships.

Story 5: Low Self-esteem and Sexual Behavior

Emily's parents divorced when she was five, and her father left home. He promised to visit her regularly, but these promises were often broken, and eventually, contact ceased altogether. Emily spent hours by the window waiting for her father to appear, but this waiting turned into a deep sense of betrayal, anger, and sadness as he never came. She internalized the belief that her father had abandoned her because she wasn't a good enough child, that she was insignificant to him, and these thoughts severely damaged her self-esteem and trust in others. As an adult, Emily finds it hard to believe that anyone will stay by her side, constantly testing her partners or seeking reassurance from them. Due to her low self-esteem and lack of trust, she struggles to set clear boundaries in relationships, sometimes using sexual behavior as a way to hold onto her partner. Although sex temporarily provides a sense of being loved, she never truly understands the concept of love or the deeper meaning behind it. Emily's low self-esteem and misunderstanding of love are rooted in her father's abandonment, leading to ongoing attachment injuries in adulthood.

Story 6: Distorted Perception of Love and Violence

Lisa grew up in a household where her father was physically and emotionally abusive. He controlled both Lisa and her mother, restricting them financially and monitoring their social relationships and outside activities. Yet, there were times when her father would cry, apologize for his actions, and promise never to hurt them again, expressing that he loved both Lisa and her mother. Lisa lived in constant fear of making her father angry but came to understand, in her distorted perception, that even his abusive behavior was a form of love. As a result, Lisa learned to equate jealousy, possessiveness, and even violence with expressions of affection. As an adult, she has very low self-esteem and is often attracted to men with dark, controlling personalities similar to her father's, frequently ending up in abusive relationships that perpetuate the cycle from her childhood. Lisa's childhood experiences taught her to associate love with control and violence, leading to severe attachment injuries that affect her relationships as an adult.

What Is the Anxious-Preoccupied Attachment Style?

"I am not worthy, and others cannot be trusted." This is a common thought pattern observed in individuals with an anxious-preoccupied attachment style. These beliefs about oneself and the world are often formed unconsciously over time. People with this attachment style tend to have a strong desire for intimacy but also a deep fear of abandonment, which significantly influences their behaviors and emotions. These fears can manifest as emotional dependency, attachment, or even possessiveness, leading to excessive suspicion, attempts to control the partner, or constant seeking of reassurance. Even when aware that their actions might be unhealthy, the intensity of their anxiety makes it difficult to suppress negative emotions and behaviors. As a result, partners may sometimes feel overwhelmed by what they perceive as "heavy" love.

Individuals with this attachment style often experience intense emotional highs and lows and tend to react strongly to perceived threats in the relationship. Their heightened sensitivity to small signs of disconnection or tension leads to frequent worry and distress, leaving little room for emotional peace. Understanding these tendencies is essential not only for the individual but also for their partner. Mutual understanding and working together on appropriate coping strategies are key to fostering a healthier relationship. Improving communication and offering emotional support can help strengthen the bond between both partners. Below are some characteristics of this attachment style:

Intense Anxiety: A pervasive fear of being abandoned or left behind in relationships.

Constant Reassurance-Seeking: A need for frequent affirmation and confirmation of love from a partner, as well as in other relationships.

Emotional Dependency: A strong reliance on the partner for emotional support and stability.

Low Self-Esteem: Persistent doubts about self-worth and whether one is deserving of love. Since self-esteem is often dependent on others' validation, it can be fragile and easily shaken.

Intense Emotional Reactions: Extreme emotional highs and lows, often experiencing either elation or deep sadness in relationships.

Impact on Other Relationships

The anxious-preoccupied attachment style can influence not only romantic relationships but also friendships, sibling relationships, and even workplace dynamics.

Friendships:

Strong Dependency: Constant anxiety leads to a need for emotional support and reassurance from friends, often causing overreactions to minor misunderstandings.

Over-Involvement: Anxious individuals may become overly involved in their friends' lives, which can come across as intrusive or overbearing.

Fear of Rejection: The fear of being abandoned can result in jealousy or possessiveness, making it difficult to tolerate a close friend forming new connections with others.

Sibling Relationships:

Pursuit of Emotional Connection: Anxious individuals often seek deep emotional bonds with siblings, needing their support and reassurance.

Conflict and Jealousy: Jealousy can arise easily, leading to frequent conflicts or rivalries between siblings.

Dependent Relationships: A desire for constant solidarity and agreement can result in overly dependent relationships with siblings.

Workplace Relationships:

Dependence on Feedback: Individuals may frequently seek feedback from supervisors or colleagues and feel uncomfortable in environments where they are expected to act independently.

Anxiety in Individual Work: There is often discomfort or anxiety around working alone, with a preference for cooperative, supportive environments.

Blurred Boundaries: Anxious individuals may form overly close relationships with coworkers, blurring the lines between personal and professional relationships, which can lead to emotional conflicts in the workplace.

Various Stages of Development

The critical period for attachment formation is typically considered to be between 6 months and 2 years of age. This is a crucial time when a child forms a strong bond with their primary caregiver (often the mother). During this period, children experience feelings of safety and trust, which lay the foundation for their social and emotional development.

According to attachment theory, the quality of attachment formed during this period has a significant impact on later relationships and psychological well-being, making appropriate care and affection essential. If attachment is not properly formed during this time, it can affect future development.

Childhood

Children with attachment difficulties may exhibit various unstable behavior patterns. Children with an anxious attachment style often feel intense anxiety about separation from their caregiver, which may manifest in crying, clinging behavior, or constant need for parental attention. In contrast, children with other insecure attachment styles may display indifference toward their caregivers or exhibit confused behaviors that mix fear and affection.

Children who have experienced severe neglect or abuse may develop profound attachment injuries and unique self-defense mechanisms. These behaviors, formed as a defense mechanism to avoid further emotional harm, are often misunderstood by those around them, as they differ greatly from the behaviors of children raised in loving environments. As a result, it becomes difficult for these children to form attachment relationships, which can lead to further isolation.

Children with severe attachment disorders may exhibit behaviors such as distancing themselves from others, building emotional walls, lying to gain attention, destroying gifts due to fear of loss, or hiding family belongings (like TV remotes) to feel a sense of security. They may also engage in secretive eating, avoiding the family's gaze. These children often have a history of moving between relatives, foster care, or residential care, with repeated experiences of changing schools. Some children may even regress to behaviors from infancy, such as intentionally having accidents, as an unconscious desire to experience early attachment relationships.

These examples represent particularly severe attachment disorders, but it is important to recognize that attachment issues, to varying degrees, can have a significant impact on a child's personality development. Early intervention through therapy is crucial for healing.

Children with attachment difficulties may also be perceived as difficult to raise, which can increase their risk of further neglect or abuse or being passed between family members. It is essential for caregivers to deeply understand the child's behavior patterns and work to prevent repeated attachment injuries. This is a vital first step in safeguarding the child's mental health and fostering healthier attachment relationships.

Adolescence

During adolescence, emotional changes and social pressures can make relationships more complex and present additional psychological challenges. This is a period that requires support and understanding, and it is especially important for adults to provide appropriate guidance.

In addition to low self-esteem, anger, and relationship issues, adolescents may become newly aware of past trauma as they undergo physical and psychological growth. This heightened awareness can result in emotional instability. Underlying beliefs like "I am unlovable," "The world is untrustworthy," or "I need to protect myself" may lead adolescents to adopt aggressive or defensive attitudes toward their caregivers or other adults. While these behaviors serve as coping mechanisms for their anxiety, they can also result in misunderstandings and conflicts.

These behavioral patterns, combined with the emotional changes and social pressures typical of adolescence, can lead to more complex relationships and mental difficulties. Therefore, it is crucial for adults to offer appropriate support during this time.

Young Adulthood

Adults with an anxious-preoccupied attachment style should take note of the following points:

Choosing Romantic Partners: It is important to understand the attachment style of potential partners to avoid unhealthy relationships, such as those involving domestic violence (DV) or emotional harm.

Improving Self-Esteem: Fostering a strong sense of self-worth that is not dependent on others' approval is essential. Activities like therapy, artistic expression, or physical exercise can help individuals spend time reflecting on themselves and build their inner self-esteem.

Respecting Sexual Boundaries: Maintaining respect for one's body and self, and consciously engaging in behaviors that enhance self-esteem, are important. Valuing oneself in this way lays the foundation for healthier relationships.

Engaging with Securely Attached Individuals: Interacting with individuals who have a secure attachment style can help internalize positive attachment behaviors and improve one's own attachment style. This can help reduce anxiety in relationships.

Avoiding Insecure Attachment Styles: It is advisable to avoid relationships with individuals who have avoidant or disorganized attachment styles, as they may cause emotional stress.

Continuing Therapy: Ongoing therapy is crucial for confronting emotional wounds and seeking healing. Professional support can greatly assist in understanding oneself and improving attachment styles.

Learning Secure Attachment: Learning and embodying a secure attachment style can have a significant impact on future parenting and marital relationships. It enhances the ability to build healthy relationships and improves interpersonal skills.

These efforts contribute to personal growth and the improvement of relationships, ultimately leading to a more stable and fulfilling life. Fostering a secure attachment style can provide a positive environment for future children and relationships, benefitting future generations as well.

Challenges in Romantic Relationships during Adulthood

Individuals with an anxious-preoccupied attachment style often face numerous challenges in romantic relationships. Fear of abandonment can lead to clingy or obsessive behaviors, which may become burdensome for their partner. Some individuals with this attachment style may also have low self-esteem and believe they are unworthy of love, which can make it difficult for them to honor and respect their own emotional and physical boundaries. In such cases, it is important for them to be mindful and take conscious steps to value and care for themselves.

There is also a tendency toward emotional highs and lows, jealousy, and possessiveness in relationships. In some instances, individuals may misinterpret abusive behavior as love, making it difficult for them to leave harmful relationships.

Addressing these challenges requires improving self-worth, managing anxiety, and developing healthy communication and coping skills. These steps can lead to more stable and balanced relationships.

Goal: Acquiring Secure Attachment Style

We've mentioned that learning and embodying a secure attachment style can have a profound impact on future parenting and marital life. To ensure that your own "attachment injuries" are not passed on to your children, it is essential to build a foundation for happy and healthy relationships for yourself.

Here are some key characteristics of a secure attachment style, which is marked by balanced interpersonal relationships and emotional stability. These characteristics are reflected in the following behaviors:

Trust in Others: Secure individuals feel comfortable relying on others and being relied upon. They trust that others will be there when needed and maintain a healthy balance of give-and-take in relationships, without always giving or always receiving.

Healthy Boundaries: They maintain a good balance between intimacy and independence, adjusting their distance in relationships based on the other person's reactions. Even if they experience anxiety, they can control and manage their emotions.

They enjoy closeness while maintaining appropriate boundaries.

Emotional Regulation: They manage their emotions well, calming feelings of anxiety or anger and handling situations rationally. Even when emotions fluctuate, they can express these feelings in words, encourage understanding, and propose solutions.

Positive Self-Image: They have healthy self-esteem, knowing they are worthy of love and capable of giving love to others. They respect their partner and their own sexuality, not being swayed by desires or pressures, and prioritizing appropriate timing and mutual consent.

Stable Relationships: They build stable and fulfilling relationships based on mutual respect, effective communication, and emotional support.

Individuals with a secure attachment style tend to report higher overall well-being. They manage stress well, experience lower levels of anxiety and depression, and feel satisfaction in their social interactions and life experiences. Cultivating a secure attachment style allows for the development of healthier, more fulfilling relationships and contributes to a more emotionally stable life.

Steps to Acquiring a Secure Attachment Style

To transition from an anxious-preoccupied attachment style to a secure attachment style, it is essential to first face and heal your emotional wounds while deepening your understanding of your inner self. Simultaneously, it is important to recognize your behavior patterns and make a conscious effort to practice secure behaviors. Below are some recommended actions and tips to guide this process:

Deepen Self-Awareness: The first step is recognizing your attachment patterns and understanding how they affect your relationships. Therapy or counseling can facilitate this process. Try keeping a journal to track feelings of anxiety or dissatisfaction, identifying specific patterns or triggers.

Increase Self-Satisfaction: Finding fulfillment and self-worth outside of relationships can reduce dependency and anxiety. Pursue hobbies or activities that bring you joy and a sense of accomplishment.

Practice Mindfulness: Mindfulness can help manage anxiety by focusing on the present moment and reducing excessive worry. Develop a habit of calming your mind through deep breathing or guided meditation practices.

Develop Effective Communication Skills: Clear communication of your needs and active listening to your partner fosters healthier relationships. Try using "active listening" techniques by repeating back what your partner says to confirm understanding.

Enhance Emotional Regulation Skills: It is important to develop skills for managing your emotions and avoiding overreactions in anxiety-provoking situations. Practice "cognitive restructuring" by reviewing distorted thoughts and reframing negative thinking that triggers anxiety into positive alternatives.

Seek Professional Support: Working with a therapist or counselor can help you learn effective strategies for cultivating a healthy attachment style. Look for attachment-focused therapies, such as Emotionally Focused Therapy (EFT) or attachment-based therapy.

Cultivate Self-Compassion: Understanding and accepting your emotions can reduce anxiety about emotional intimacy. Try self-compassion exercises, such as writing yourself a letter from the perspective of a close friend.

By continuing to practice these strategies, individuals with anxious-preoccupied or avoidant attachment styles can move toward a secure attachment style, ultimately building healthier, more satisfying relationships.

Transitioning to a Secure Attachment Style

The first step in transitioning is to recognize your current attachment style and understand how it impacts your relationships and overall emotional well-being. Reflecting on past experiences, particularly your relationship with caregivers during childhood, is essential for uncovering the root of your anxious-preoccupied tendencies. Therapy can support this process by providing a safe space to explore your emotions deeply and better understand your attachment patterns.

Building Trust and Emotional Independence

A crucial aspect of transitioning to a secure attachment style is developing trust and fostering emotional independence. This means learning to stabilize your emotions without relying on constant reassurance from others. Individuals with an anxious-preoccupied style often fear abandonment and continually seek affirmation of love. To improve this tendency, it is effective to practice self-soothing techniques and engage in activities that help you recognize your own value. Building relationships with people who offer stable and reliable support is also essential. Positive experiences in relationships strengthen your ability to feel valued without the need for constant validation.

Effective Communication and Self-Compassion

Effective communication and cultivating self-compassion are key to transitioning to a secure attachment style. Those with an anxious-preoccupied style may overly depend on their partner's reactions when expressing emotions and needs. To address this, it is important to learn how to communicate feelings clearly and assertively. For example, using active listening techniques and "I-statements" can help foster understanding and reduce reliance on others for emotional validation.

Self-compassion is equally important. Recognizing that anxiety-driven behaviors were once adaptive responses to past experiences can help individuals avoid self-blame. Developing self-compassion reduces self-criticism and enhances self-worth, which lays the foundation for a more secure attachment style.

Gradual Process

Transitioning to a secure attachment style is a gradual process that requires patience and consistent effort. However, by experiencing positive relationships, fostering a positive self-image, and building emotional stability, individuals with an anxious-preoccupied style can cultivate more satisfying and emotionally connected relationships. Through this process, they can slowly move toward a healthier, more secure attachment style.

Traits of Ideal Partner and Red Flags

For individuals with an anxious-preoccupied attachment style, certain types of partners can provide reassurance and stability, while others may exacerbate their feelings of insecurity. This section describes the characteristics of an ideal partner, the types of individuals to be cautious about, and those who may present a "learning relationship" that requires mutual growth and understanding.

Being Okay Without a Partner

People with anxious attachment tendencies often assess their self-worth based on others' evaluations, making it difficult to endure being without a partner. This loneliness can lead them to quickly engage with people who approach them, often rapidly escalating relationships. However, caution is necessary.

Without cultivating self-confidence and the ability to enjoy life independently, it becomes impossible to properly evaluate a potential partner. It is essential to first focus on activities you enjoy—such as exercise or artistic pursuits—and strengthen your communication with same-gender friends who are not romantic interests. This helps foster a mindset where you can confidently enjoy life, even without a romantic partner.

Characteristics of an Ideal Partner

This doesn't mean you should dismiss everyone who approaches you until you've fully developed a strong sense of self-worth. Of course, when someone wonderful comes along, it's important to experience the joy of a happy relationship. However, if your emotional wounds haven't fully healed or you haven't transitioned to a secure attachment style, you need to carefully assess your partner.

This is because your partner's attachment style can influence your own. Even if you are committed to building a healthy relationship, if your partner is emotionally unstable, it may become challenging.

The ideal partner for someone with an anxious attachment style is, of course, someone with a secure attachment style. Engaging with such individuals allows you to learn new ways of building relationships. However, there are cases where people who appear secure may have hidden attachment insecurities. These tendencies may be well-masked, and it might take considerable time to notice their instability. While there is no foolproof method for identifying this early, here are some characteristics of ideal and avoidable partners:

Ideal Partner Traits

Provides Reassurance: Consistently offers reassurance, helping to ease fears of abandonment.

Emotionally Expressive: Openly expresses their feelings and regularly communicates love and commitment.

Stable and Reliable: Acts consistently, providing a sense of security through dependable behavior.

Emotionally Stable: Generally, manages emotions such as anger or anxiety well, with the ability to process and control these feelings.

Attentive and Caring: Responds to the partner's needs and engages in the relationship with genuine care and effort.

Patient and Understanding: Understands and supports their partner through emotional waves, while gently encouraging emotional independence.

Recognizing the Red Flags

Not all challenging relationships are inherently negative. If both partners can learn from each other, and take the path to fostering a strong relationship, then the relationship can still be valuable. However, individuals with an anxious attachment style should be particularly cautious of falling into abusive relationships, where they may struggle to escape. Below are characteristics of a "learning relationship" partner:

Emotionally Unstable: A person who lacks consistency in their behavior and is unreliable may heighten fears of abandonment.

Emotionally Unavailable: Someone who struggles to express their emotions may increase anxiety in an anxious-preoccupied partner.

Ignores Partner's Anxiety: A person who dismisses or neglects their partner's need for reassurance and affection may exacerbate feelings of insecurity.

Indifferent: An emotionally indifferent partner who cannot respond to their partner's needs intensifies fears of being left behind.

Avoidant: Someone who avoids serious conversations about commitment or the relationship can create instability for an anxious-preoccupied partner.

Has Attachment-Related Trauma: While some people with traumatic experiences can develop a secure attachment style, others may struggle, leading to a more challenging relationship dynamic.

Even in relationships with these partners, if both individuals are willing to communicate and support each other's growth, there is potential for the relationship to evolve into a more secure attachment style. In any relationship, cooperation, growth, and healing are the ideal outcomes.

Caution: If you have experienced physical or emotional abuse, it is important to focus on your safety rather than hoping that "they will change someday." If your partner has deep emotional wounds, the abusive behavior will not stop until they resolve their own issues.

Parenting Tips

Children with an anxious-preoccupied attachment style require constant reassurance and support. This behavior does not indicate a lack of love or trust in their parents; rather, it stems from past experiences and how their attachment was formed. Below are ways to better understand and support these children.

Listen to Them

As a caregiver for a child with attachment injuries, the first thing to consider is what you can do as a parent to help them build a secure attachment style. Expecting good results in areas like academics, while the child remains in an unstable emotional state, can be challenging. This is because when they feel anxiety, fear, or anger, their survival brain is activated, which hinders the functioning of the prefrontal cortex—the part of the brain responsible for intellectual activities.

One of the most effective ways to provide reassurance and foster attachment is simply to *listen*. Being heard makes people feel understood and valued. Therefore, no matter how small the issue may seem, pause whatever you are doing and listen to them with your heart and full attention.

Speak Calmly

Like any child, children with anxious attachment styles will make mistakes. At times, it will be necessary to set rules and discipline. However, pay particular attention to the tone of your voice. Children, especially those with experiences of abuse, may perceive rules as an unfair tool of control by adults and may quickly become defiant. Thus, it's important to calmly explain that rules are in place to protect both parties and help them understand. This process may require patience and repetition.

Communicate Effectively

Building a healthy relationship with children who have anxious-preoccupied attachment styles requires clear and empathetic communication. Creating a space where emotional needs can be openly discussed allows the child to feel that their emotions are understood. In discipline or rule-setting discussions, it's important to avoid approaches that make the child feel defensive. Children will only begin to accept adult guidance and reflect it in their behavior when they feel understood.

Avoid using phrases like "You're wrong," which trigger defensive responses and make the child focus on crafting excuses instead of correcting their behavior. For instance, aggressive tones or unexplained punishments fall into this category. When children face this approach, they focus on making excuses rather than feeling motivated to change. Additionally, some parents may resort to criticizing the child's character, hoping it will lead to better behavior, but this often has the opposite effect, making parenting more difficult.

Instead of saying, "You're wrong," express your feelings by saying, "I feel this way about your behavior." This conveys your emotions without blaming the child and helps foster better understanding.

Listen with Empathy

As mentioned earlier, children will only begin to listen to their parents when they feel understood. Even if the child shares something that seems trivial to the parent, consistently paying attention to those small moments helps the child feel, "I am valued" and "My thoughts and feelings matter." This is the foundation for building healthy self-esteem and secure attachment relationships.

By listening, parents also help children develop emotional regulation skills and emotional expression, contributing to higher emotional intelligence (EQ).

EQ, often regarded as more important than IQ for living a happy life, helps children navigate their emotions and interactions.

Children with higher levels of anxiety can learn to manage their worries through their parents' empathetic responses. Make sure to create an environment where the child feels safe expressing their emotions and concerns.

Building Trust and Safety

Establishing trust and creating an emotionally safe environment is essential. Trust is built when parents respond consistently and behave predictably. Responding to the child's need for reassurance each time it arises, discussing situations in advance, or reassuring them by calling or using FaceTime when separated can gradually reduce their anxiety. It's crucial not to downplay their anxiety and to consistently respond to their need for reassurance. Additionally, when the child takes small steps toward emotional independence, praise them to reinforce the behavior, thereby motivating further positive actions. Be patient and supportive as they grow.

Fostering Self-Reflection and Growth

Encouraging self-reflection is crucial in helping children with an anxious-preoccupied attachment style foster healthy psychological development. By exploring their attachment patterns and supporting their emotional growth, we can facilitate their transition to a more secure attachment style.

Encouraging Self-Awareness: Help the child understand the background of their anxieties and emotions and take steps to foster self-growth.

Independently Sufficient Self-Esteem: Encourage activities like journaling or mindfulness to promote self-reflection, and support them in pursuing art, sports, or other passions. Celebrate each small success along the way. These practices help build a strong foundation of self-esteem that is not reliant on external validation.

Maintaining the Parent's Emotional Well-Being

Supporting a child with an anxious-preoccupied attachment style can be emotionally demanding for the parent as well. It is important for the parent to prioritize their own emotional health and seek support when needed.

Maintain Emotional Balance: Parents should consider seeking support from friends or a therapist to avoid emotional exhaustion.

Set Healthy Boundaries: Pay attention to your own emotional needs and support your child without overextending yourself.

Raising a child with an anxious-preoccupied attachment style can be challenging, but with consistent support and by creating an emotionally safe environment, it is possible to help the child develop a more secure attachment.

Advice for Romantic Partners

Being in a relationship with someone who has an anxious-preoccupied attachment style requires efforts to provide reassurance. These individuals often have a deep fear of abandonment, which leads them to frequently seek validation of love. This behavior doesn't indicate a lack of trust or love in your relationship but stems from underlying fears and anxieties. As a partner, it's important to understand this and offer support to build a stable and secure relationship.

Be Patient

Your partner may frequently seek reassurance and confirmation of love because they fear being abandoned. Patience is key in responding to these behaviors. During emotionally sensitive periods, offering reassurance and remaining calm can help ease their anxiety.

Provide Consistent Support

Partners with an anxious-preoccupied attachment style often need emotional support and frequent validation of love. For them, stability and predictability are extremely important. By consistently demonstrating reliable and trustworthy behavior, you can reduce their anxiety and build a more stable relationship.

Encourage Emotional Independence

While providing reassurance, it's also important to gradually encourage your partner to develop emotional independence. Supporting them in building self-sufficiency and recognizing their own worth can reduce dependency. Offering positive feedback when they take independent actions or achieve personal goals can be very effective.

Maintain Open and Honest Communication

Partners with an anxious-preoccupied attachment style may sometimes experience insecurity about the relationship. Encourage open and honest communication rather than suppressing these feelings. Respect their emotions and seek to understand them without dismissing their concerns. At the same time, express your own feelings and needs honestly to foster a more balanced relationship.

Consider Couple's Therapy

In some cases, seeking professional support together can be beneficial for the partnership. Couples therapy provides an effective way to better understand each other's attachment styles and communication patterns, ultimately strengthening the relationship.

Personal Growth and Support as a Partner

To maintain a healthy relationship with a partner who has an anxious-preoccupied attachment style, it's essential to support your partner while also prioritizing your own emotional health. Maintaining your own emotional well-being is crucial for sustaining the relationship, and seeking support when needed is important. A relationship where both partners grow together and support each other is key to long-term success.

How to Enhance Self-Esteem

Building Self-Esteem from Within

Basing your self-worth on others' evaluations is not a healthy pattern, as it requires constant attention to how others perceive you. Others' reactions are often unpredictable and not always positive, making externally based self-esteem as fragile as a house built on sand. For individuals with an anxious attachment style, cultivating self-esteem from within is the first step to growth. It's important to become aware of your behaviors, emotions, and thought patterns, and how they impact your relationships and daily life. Here are some specific steps to enhance your self-esteem:

Increase Emotional Awareness

Becoming more sensitive to your emotions is a crucial first step in building self-esteem. Pay attention to the emotions you experience in everyday life and observe what situations or events trigger them. Keep a daily emotional journal, noting the emotions you felt strongly and what triggered them. Recognizing common emotions like anger, anxiety, joy, and calm can help you identify patterns.

Reflect on Past Experiences

Your attachment style is heavily influenced by childhood experiences and relationships with family members. Reflecting on these past events can help you understand how they are affecting your current relationships. Write down important past events, relationships with parents or siblings, and explore how these experiences influence your current relationships.

Ask Self-Reflective Questions

To better understand your behaviors and thought patterns, ask yourself questions that promote self-discovery. Consider questions like:

- "When do I feel the most anxious or secure?"
- "What patterns do I repeat in my relationships?"
- "What expectations do I have of my partner or friends?"
- "How much do I rely on others for my
- emotional well-being?"

Use Self-Assessment Tools

Using tools like self-assessment questionnaires can help you objectively evaluate your tendencies and patterns. Based on the results, you can identify areas for improvement and change. Use the attachment style assessment included in this book to learn more about your attachment style and how it influences your relationships.

Make Self-Reflection a Habit

By regularly setting aside time for self-reflection, you can track your growth and changes, leading to a deeper understanding of yourself. Be mindful of your emotions and behaviors and deepen your self-awareness. Create a weekly habit of reflecting on your emotions, thoughts, and behaviors. Record what went well and where improvements can be made.

Seek Feedback

Getting external perspectives on your behaviors and emotions can also help enhance your self-esteem. Actively seek feedback from trusted friends, family, or a therapist. Ask close ones how they perceive you and what patterns they notice, using their input to gain a broader understanding of yourself.

Seek Professional Support

Counseling or therapy is a highly effective way to enhance self-esteem. Through professional guidance, you can gain deeper insights into your attachment style and behavioral patterns. Consider using therapy that specializes in attachment styles and emotional well-being, such as attachment-based therapy or cognitive behavioral therapy, to further develop self-esteem.

By following these steps, you can deepen your self-awareness, understand your emotions and behaviors more fully, and build a solid foundation for healthier, more stable relationships.

Final Thoughts

As you reach the end of this book, I hope the journey has provided you with insight, comfort, and a deeper understanding of yourself and your relationships. The pages you've turned are not just about learning, but about growth, healing, and finding your own path to emotional well-being. Remember, the process of self-discovery is ongoing, and every step you take brings you closer to a more fulfilling, connected life.

You are worthy of love, peace, and happiness. May the knowledge you've gained here serve as a gentle reminder of your strength and potential. Keep moving forward with kindness toward yourself, and know that healing is always possible, no matter where you are on your journey.

Thank you for allowing this book to be a part of your life. I wish you all the best in your continued journey towards wholeness and joy.

With warmest regards,

Emiko Chibana

Made in United States
Orlando, FL
06 December 2024

55064176R00036